Family Life Illustrated

for MARRIAGE

RONNIE FLOYD

Family Life Illustrated

For MARRIAGE

RONNIE FLOYD

New Leaf Press

Family Life Illustrated for Marriage

First printing: November 2004

ISBN: 0-89221-585-2
Library of Congress Number: 2004106957

Cover concept by Left Coast Design, Portland, OR

All sidebar statistics have been provided by: The Barna Group
Online, 1957 Eastman Ave Ste B, Ventura, CA 93003.
(www.barna.org/FlexPage.aspx?Page=Topic&TopicID=20)

Printed in the United States of America

Please visit our website for other great titles:
www.newleafpress.net

For information regarding author interviews,
please contact the publicity department
at (870) 438-5288.

CONTENTS

Winning the Marriage Game

YOUR own experience is unique. Looking longingly down that aisle, you saw the most beautiful bride in the world. Or, taking your father's arm, you caught a glimpse of a handsome groom.

Whether you are a man reading this book, or a woman who opened its pages, you probably know something about being married. But do you know very much about being in

a blissful marriage? Is it better than at the beginning? Or have the years dulled things a bit?

Marriage was ordained by God, and His word is our model for all relationships, including the all-important union of two souls. As you read this book, it is my hope that the *biblical* model for success comes through. In this age of self-help, secularism, and "me-ism," how

refreshing are the pages of Scripture, lighting the way to marital bliss, even if it isn't all candlelight and soft music.

It has been my intent to look at what Scripture tells us about marrying well. Forget the latest cure-all for a troubled marriage. Put the magazine articles on a shelf. Turn off the talk-show queens and kings. For it is in the Bible that we find solutions for sagging marriages; tips for keeping it all fresh; and proper attitudes for both husbands and wives.

If you don't communicate well, there's something here for you. If the romance is less-than-desirable, have a read. If decisions have become acrimonious, consider Family Life Illustrated for Marriage. Learn about God's timing vs. our timing; priorities, the "4:32 rules," and much more. Decades of marriage have made me appreciate my bride even more, and it is my sincere, fervent desire for you to *love* walking in the door of your marriage every day!

Marriage can be hard work, but it was ordained by God, and is therefore rewarding, exciting, and a wonderful privilege. You have a choice in how you see your marriage. You can view it from a humanistic, "me-first" mindset, or you can see it as the biblical model: selfless and Christ-centered.

It is my hope that you will make Jesus Christ the center of your union.

Whether your marriage is thriving, or drowning, Jesus is unchanging, and more than willing to bless and prosper you and your spouse.

> *It is my hope that you will make Jesus Christ the center of your union.*

"Married life is a marathon.
. . . It is not enough to make
a great start toward long-
term marriage. You will need
the determination to keep
plugging. . . . Only then will
you make it to the end."

- James Dobson

Chapter 1

The Revelation of Marriage

MARRIAGE is a revelation — and I'm not talking only about the Bible's revelation on marriage (which we'll get to in just a moment). Kids have their own revelations regarding marriage, and some of them just might keep you awake at night.

Someone asked Kirsten, age ten, how people decide whom they should marry.

"No person really decides before they grow up who they're going to marry," Kirsten replied. "God decides it all way before, and you get to find out later who you're stuck with."

Alan, also aged ten, had a much less theological take on the question, but his answer may not bring you any more comfort than what Kirsten had

need a solid revelation to build upon. Fortunately, we have exactly that in God's Word, the Bible. For there the Creator of marriage gives us His authoritative take on what it means to be married and how we can best make this holy union between a man and a woman work, grow, and flourish.

The Master's View

One day a group of Jesus' most frequent opponents approached him with a loaded question. They tried to get him in trouble with a query about divorce, but Jesus responded with an answer focused primarily on marriage. Here's how Matthew records the incident:

to say. "You got to find somebody who likes the same stuff," he declared. "Like, if you like sports, she should like it that you like sports, and she should keep the chips and dip coming."

While childish revelations may keep us laughing, in order to build a solid marriage that honors God and blesses others, we

The Pharisees also came to Jesus, testing Him and saying to Him, "Is it lawful for a man to divorce his wife for just any reason?" And He answered and said to them, "Have you not read that He made them at the beginning made them male and female, and said, 'For this reason, man shall leave his father and mother and be joined to his wife, and the two shall be become one flesh?' And so then there are no longer two but one flesh. Therefore, what God has joined together, let not man separate" (Matt. 19:3–6).

Even when asked about divorce, Jesus immediately pointed back to the origin of marriage. That's very important to note. Jesus urged his opponents to go back to the original blueprint for marriage, found in the book of Genesis. Consider the three key Scriptures Jesus referenced:

> *We will get nowhere until we recognize that marriage is God's idea.*

So God created man in His own image; in the image of God He created him; male and female He created them (Gen. 1:27).

Therefore a man shall leave his father and mother and be joined to his wife, and they shall become one flesh (Gen. 2:24).

In the day that God created man, He made him in the likeness of God. He created them male and female, and blessed them and called them Mankind in the day they were created (Gen. 5:1–2).

By alluding to these foundational passages, Jesus was in essence saying, "You don't need to worry about what kind of divorce is permissible or under what circumstances God sanctions your desire to get out of a marriage. It's not even going to be a question if you are working on your marriage, as God has commanded, and you are trying to make your marriage into all that God wants it to be." Jesus' opponents focused on the question of divorce; Jesus focused on the answer of marriage.

So what did Jesus teach us about marriage? He highlighted at least three things in this passage.

1. Marriage is a God-appointed union.

We will get nowhere until we recognize that marriage is *God's* idea. It is not an institution created by society or through human ingenuity, as some would claim today. The Word of God places the Lord of the universe squarely at the center of all discussion on marriage. The Bible makes it clear that the great and holy God of glory is the originator of marriage. It was His idea. He's the one who mandated it. He's the one who designed it. *God* is the one who appoints marriage.

This tells me that I

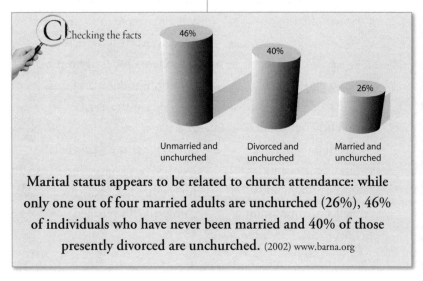

Checking the facts

46%

40%

26%

Unmarried and unchurched

Divorced and unchurched

Married and unchurched

Marital status appears to be related to church attendance: while only one out of four married adults are unchurched (26%), 46% of individuals who have never been married and 40% of those presently divorced are unchurched. (2002) www.barna.org

didn't marry my wife, Jeana, by coincidence. I didn't marry Jeana because I'm the only available man that she could find. I married Jeana by divine appointment. God brought us together and God made us into one flesh.

This idea still floors me. How in the world could a little west Texas girl ever meet and fall in love with a little south Texas boy? How could God ever bring the two together?

In human terms, it's called "college." It's called "experience." It's called "running the race." And one day when we were each separately running the race, we looked around and saw one another also running the race. We met, started talking, fell in love, and came to believe that God

> God *is the one who appoints marriage.*

was putting us together. When we finally walked down the aisle to become Mr. and Mrs. Floyd, we simply culminated the process that God had begun. Our marriage is a God-appointed union — and if you're married, so is yours.

Don't forget what Jesus said: "What *God* has joined together. . . ." Did a human minister perform our wedding ceremony? Sure. Did the state recognize our union? Definitely. Did our wedding guests, by their very presence, endorse our marriage? Certainly. But don't get confused — *God* is the central player here. It was *God* who joined us together. Not the minister. Not the state. Not our friends or community. *God.*

> *Marriage is not merely a piece of paper that contractually binds one person to another.*

2. Marriage is a physical union.

The Bible tells us that a husband and his wife are "one flesh." That means that, beyond all doubt, marriage is a physical union.

And with that in mind, I'd like to offer you a mathematics lesson.

First, I admit that math is one of my worst subjects. I am good at adding, multiplying and dividing (and whatever that other one is, oh yes, subtraction). I'm just not very good at any thing like algebra, geometry, or anything that is beyond the basics of mathematics. If you keep it very basic, then maybe I understand; but otherwise, forget it.

On the other hand, I am very good at divine mathematics. In fact, I have a degree in divine mathematics. May I show you a prime example of divine mathematics? Here it is: one plus one equals one. Even I can get that one.

Jesus insisted that, in marriage, one man plus one woman equals one flesh. Marriage is many things, but without question it is a physical union.

When a man and a woman come together under God to get married, they immediately form a physical union — in heaven's eyes, it's impossible to know where one begins and the other ends. They are "one flesh."

This is the kind of marriage that God wants for every one of us. We are to think of ourselves, not as two separate individuals who think fondly of the "other half," but as a unit, as a team, as one flesh united by God and for God's purposes.

Marriage is not merely a piece of paper that contractually binds one person to another. It is not simply one of many kinds of relationships. Marriage is a physical union that unites two people into one. That helps to explain why divorce hurts so much; in a divorce, men are tearing apart what God has made into one flesh. How could that not hurt?

3. Marriage is a permanent union.

Jesus said very clearly, "What God has joined together, let no man separate." That means that God intends marriage to be permanent.

He never endorsed "serial marriage," in which people feel very free to flit from one marriage partner to another.

Of course, it is very obvious today that marriage is not considered permanent by a huge percentage of people, both inside and outside the church. Too many of us have adopted the bogus creed, "God wants me to be happy," and have made that creed the top concern of our lives. Therefore, as soon as we don't "feel happy" in our marriage, we take it as a divine right that we should be able to divorce our spouse and look for someone better, someone more able to give us the happiness that has eluded us.

Jesus rejects any such foolish notion. Nowhere does He say, "Since God wants you to be happy, go ahead and divorce your spouse so that you can look for someone who can make you happier." In fact, He says nothing of the sort. What He does say is something quite different from that: "What God has joined together, let no man separate" (Matt. 19:6).

Could He be any clearer? Jesus intends marriage to be permanent.

Just as there is no such thing as "gay marriage" and no such thing as "group marriage," so there is no such thing as "trial marriage." Jesus could not have made himself any more plain on this point. He taught that marriage is a permanent union between a man and a woman. God designed it that way, and He's never seen the need to redesign it into something else.

It's Just the Beginning

A few years before he died, Bible scholar Kenneth Kantzer wrote a column for *Christianity Today* that touched on some of the lessons his 50 years of marriage had taught him. He ended his column with the thoughts below, and I'd like to end this chapter by piggybacking on his comments. They're worth pondering — especially today.

Corrie ten Boom was right:

"The growth of the Christian life

> *"What God has joined together, let no man separate"* *(Matt. 19:6).*

does not stop at the first surrender any more than marriage stops at the wedding ceremony." Getting married is obviously not the end of marriage. It is only the beginning.

Several years ago while shopping in the local supermarket, my wife chatted briefly with the checker at the counter. She happened to mention that we were celebrating our 48th wedding anniversary.

"My," exclaimed the girl, "I don't think I could ever find a man I'd be willing to live with for 48 years."

"Well," responded my wife, "Don't you ever get married until you do find one."

And that is good advice.

Fifty years is a long time for two people to live together. But for us, each year is better than the one before. And we are thankful to God.[1]

Endnotes

1 Kenneth S. Kantzer, "The Freedom of Jealousy," *Christianity Today* (October 21, 1988): p. 11.

> *"The growth of the Christian life does not stop at the first surrender any more than marriage stops at the wedding ceremony."*

Do you and your spouse feed each other a steady diet of put-downs? If you do, your marriage could be headed for divorce court. When psychologists Cliff Nortarius and Howard Markman studied newlyweds over the first decade of marriage, they discovered that couples who stayed together uttered 5 or fewer put-downs in every 100 comments to each other. But couples who inflicted twice as many verbal wounds — 10 or more putdowns out of every 100 comments — later split up. Watch what you say! Little, nit-picking comments are like a cancer in marriage, slowly draining the life out of a committed relationship.

– Dr. James Dobson's Focus on the Family Bulletin,
May, 1994

Chapter 2

Three Characteristics of a Healthy Marriage

The guests who attended an August 2001 wedding reception for Kathy and Larry Naylor must have wondered what they had gotten themselves into — and, perhaps even more so, what the bride and groom had gotten themselves into. Everyone learned pretty quickly that there's a big difference between a marriage and a healthy marriage.

The trouble started just a few hours after the couple's Sunday afternoon wedding, held in the back yard of their Homosassa, Florida, mobile home. Although the pair had taken some precautions — "I told everyone I didn't want any fighting at my wedding. You know the rednecks around here," said

Larry — a couple of guests got into a spat while the Budweiser flowed freely, and the groom tried to intervene.

Some time later, the newly married Kathy Naylor showed up to confront the girlfriend of the young man whom she thought had started the conflict. According to police reports, she kicked in the door and the two women began fighting; in the scuffle, Naylor got whacked with the phone that her antagonist was using to dial 911. Police arrested Naylor on one count of battery and she spent the night at the Citrus County jail. The next day, her new husband used their honeymoon money to bail her out (they had planned to use the funds for a trip to Busch Gardens in Tampa).[1]

Married? Sure. But a healthy marriage? That's a different question altogether.

We'd all be a lot better off if we remembered what a huge difference there is between a marriage and a healthy marriage. Nobody gets married in the hope that their union will give them loads of pain and heartache. Everyone who walks down the aisle wants to be happy, to have a successful partnership, to enjoy a grand adventure together. Unfortunately, however, less than 50 percent of the couples that marry today stay together long enough to achieve their marital dreams.

Why?

One huge reason is that they fail to take into account God's design for a healthy marriage. And that's a blunder that none of us who are married can afford to make.

Proverbs 5:15–19 outlines three biblical characteristics of a healthy marriage. When all three of these characteristics flourish in the relationship between a husband and a wife, the chances are pretty high that it will earn the label of "healthy" — and so enjoy the benefits that such a delightful union brings.

The Necessity of Commitment

No marriage can grow strong and healthy without the biblical ingredient of commitment. So the Word of God tells us, "Drink water from your

No marriage can grow strong and healthy without the biblical ingredient of commitment.

own cistern and running water from your own well. Should your fountains be dispersed abroad, streams of water in the streets? Let them be only your own and not for strangers with you. Let your fountain be blessed and rejoice with the wife of your youth" (Prov. 5:15–18).

These verses describe a commitment to fidelity, a dedication to marital faithfulness. In these words God calls men to remain faithful to their spouse.

Did you notice the imagery in the text? The passage says, "Drink water from your own cistern and running water from your own well." In other words, don't go looking for sexual or physical refreshment anywhere else but at home.

Drink deeply from your own cistern and your own well. Don't even take a sip from someone else's cistern or well.

The word "fountain" alludes to a man's reproductive powers. So the writer asks, "Should your reproductive powers be dispersed abroad?" Obviously, he expects only one answer: "No!"

How would you answer the writer's question? Are you drinking only from your own cistern? Are you enjoying only your own well? Are you dispersing abroad your reproductive powers?

In other words, are you a man (or woman) committed to fidelity? You will be if you want a healthy marriage.

The writer also warns the reader not to disperse his "streams of water" in "the streets." And just who would be walking the streets? Prostitutes. So he warns men who want healthy marriages to stay away from prostitutes — it sounds simple and obvious enough, but thousands of men destroy their marriages every year by failing to heed his obvious advice.

Husbands and wives who want a healthy marriage have to remain committed to each other. Commitment has to stand at the top of the heap. You won't get anywhere without it. We are to give ourselves and our reproductive powers only to our mate.

If you want a healthy marriage — if you want to be blessed by God in your home and in your family — then listen to what God says: "Rejoice with the wife of your youth." The idea is not that a man should have a young wife, or even that he ought to marry at a young age, but rather that he remain married to the same woman he wed when he first said, "I do." And he's not merely to stay married; he's to "rejoice" with her. That means that the kind of commitment God calls us to in marriage is not a hard, humorless, duty-bound kind of obligation empty of all color and warmth. Rather, it's a commitment that laughs easily, a commitment that smiles broadly, a commitment that has a good time.

And in fact, who has a better time than a couple

> *Husbands and wives who want a healthy marriage have to remain committed to each other.*

who has remained together through thick and thin and who has expressed and lived out a mutual commitment to tackle life together? Consider what the late Norman Vincent Peale once wrote in a *Guideposts* article titled, "Worth Fighting For":

I can speak about marriage with conviction because,

having been married for over forty years to the same wonderful woman, I can testify that there is nothing else like the closeness, the mutual support, the deep affection and companionship that grow between a man and a woman who have fought the battles of life together for years and years. Pleasures are brighter because you share them. Problems are lighter because you face them together. There's no describing these things, really; you have to experience them to know them. And the only way to experience them is to set one shining goal in marriage, permanence, and stick to it no matter what adversities you may encounter along the way.[2]

"Permanence" comes through faithfulness, and faithfulness blooms in the rich soil of commitment. Make sure you have plenty of it in your garden.

> *Does it surprise you to learn that God thinks there must be attraction in the best of marriages?*

The Necessity of Attraction

Does it surprise you to learn that God thinks there must be attraction in the best of marriages? Proverbs 5:19 declares, "As a loving deer and as a graceful doe, let her breasts satisfy you at all times. And always be enraptured with her love."

When I preached a message on this text at my church, several sleepy teenage boys in the back of the sanctuary suddenly woke up after I read this verse. Yes, Scripture really does talk about feeling attracted to your mate!

The writer uses the picture of the deer and the doe to illustrate something very important. These animals make great illustrations because of their natural grace and speed. They possess an elegant beauty in their form and eyes and even in their movement. Do you see the picture God is painting? He says that, in healthy marriages, both partners see things in the other that create powerful feelings of attraction.

The Bible tells husbands that the breasts of their wives are to satisfy them "at all times." It says, "Let her breasts satisfy you at all times," not, "Let another woman's breasts satisfy you." This isn't a pick and choose deal — sometimes you enjoy your spouse, at other times you enjoy someone else. It's an exclusive attractiveness that you are to guard at all costs.

Some people get nervous when we start talking

about physical attractiveness as a spiritual concern, but they really shouldn't. The Bible wouldn't mention it if it weren't important. I bring this up because I think we can make a bad mistake in the church on this subject if we're not careful. We can build the impression in the minds of young adults that if they feel attracted to someone, that's somehow bad and sinful. No, it's not! God made us with a desire to look at the opposite sex. The key is to keep those desires within proper boundaries. And so long as we keep those desires within the boundaries set by Scripture, there is no sin in it.

Do you remember the powerful story about Jacob, described

in Genesis 29? The first time Jacob saw Rachel, he kissed her. And then he spoke to her. And then he wept — not because she slapped him for being fresh, but because he felt overcome with attraction to her and gratitude to the faithfulness of God.

Why did he feel attracted to her? It's very simple: the Bible says that her "form and appearance" drew him to her. In other words, she was one hot babe!

(At this point in the same message that woke up those sleepy teenagers, I saw yet another teenage boy look anxiously to his friend and ask, "What chapter was that?")

So you see, there is physical attraction. God wants the male to feel

God made us with a desire to look at the opposite sex.

attracted to the female and the female attracted to the male. It's okay; in fact, it's more than just okay; it's very good. Too many of us have such a distorted view of sexuality that we're shaming people when they don't need to be shamed.

Author and psychologist Nathaniel Branden says that couples who stay together and who create healthy homes have several things in common, among them:

THREE CHARACTERISTICS OF A HEALTHY MARRIAGE

They are physically affectionate. Loving couples indulge in hand-holding, hugging, and cuddling. "An infant first experiences love through touch. We never outgrow that need," one husband said.

They express their love sexually. Sex remains vital for them long after the first passionate years of a relationship have passed. This does not mean they regard sex as the most significant aspect of their marriage. And there are great variations in frequency of lovemaking among happy couples. Yet the expression, "With my body I thee worship" is one they understand and practice. Sex, for these couples, is integrated with feelings of love and caring.[3]

Is physical intimacy and sex within marriage, a spiritual concern? You bet it is. That's why the apostle Paul could write, "Let the

> *Is physical intimacy and sex within marriage, a spiritual concern? You bet it is.*

husband render to this wife the affection due her, and likewise also the wife to her husband. The wife does not have authority over her own body, but the husband does. And likewise the husband does not have authority over his own body, but the wife does. Do not deprive one another except with consent for a time, that you may give yourselves to fasting and prayer; and come together again so that Satan does not tempt you because of your lack of self-control" (1 Cor. 7:3–5).

If you want a healthy marriage, you'll treat the physical part of your relationship as an important spiritual concern. You can't afford to do otherwise.

The Necessity of Ecstasy

You might not anticipate the third characteristic of a healthy marriage as described in Proverbs 5: ecstasy. Consider verse 19: "And always be enraptured with her love." The Scripture calls husbands and wives to continually nurture feelings of delight in the love of their spouse.

Maybe you've been married for 20 years. Can you say you're still enraptured with your spouse? Or perhaps you've been married 15 years . . . or 10 . . . or just 5. I'll ask the same question of you. Are you still enraptured with the spouse of your youth? If you want a healthy marriage, you'll take pains to encourage this third characteristic.

The word translated "enraptured" means to be in ecstasy. It means that you feel rapturous delight and overwhelmingly positive emotion in the presence of your mate. That feeling is so powerful that it can become ecstatic, beyond all reason and all logic.

Do you ever feel this kind of potent emotion in the presence of your spouse? Or have you allowed things to cool to such a degree that you wouldn't know ecstasy if it reached out and bit you on the nose?

As we've seen, healthy marriages are based on commitment, but that commitment is not some cold, bloodless decision that lacks the power to excite one's emotions. Neither am I talking about continual fireworks and perpetual volcanoes of love. Yet for a marriage to become truly healthy, there must be ecstasy — and often, it comes in places you might not expect.

Author Dale Hanson Bourke once wrote,

> The real romance in my marriage is made up of the big and little gestures we've made over the years as we've learned to accommodate and enjoy each other's particular wants and needs.

The times Tom has gone shopping with me and I've gone to see science fiction movies with him. The appreciation I now have of automotive developments and the interest he's taken in Chinese cooking. The fact that I let him pick out our dishes and he let me choose the curtains.

These are the moments that have knit us together over the years, and if Tom never brought me flowers again, or if I continued to wear my red terry bathrobe until it was even more ragged than it is, there would still be romance in our marriage.[4]

> *Yet for a marriage to become truly healthy, there must be ecstasy . . .*

Do you know why there would still be romance? Because Dale and Tom know better than to let the embers of their emotion for one another go dark and cold. And so they take practical steps to keep it alive and hot and glowing — not necessarily fireworks or volcanoes every night, but at least a comfy spot in front of the fireplace.

That'll work. And it will work for you, too.

THREE CHARACTERISTICS OF A HEALTHY MARRIAGE

Old, but Good, Advice

Almost 500 years ago, Martin Luther gave some famous advice about marriage that still holds up well today. He told his listeners, "Let the wife make the husband glad to come home, and let him make her sorry to see him leave."

It would be pretty hard to follow his good advice, though, without commitment. It would be pretty difficult to make it work without attraction. And it would be a tough assignment to pull off without ecstasy.

But are all three of those biblical characteristics at work and growing in your marriage? Then you're well on your way to a healthy marriage. And you'll have the grins and good times to prove it.

Endnotes

1 Carrie Johnson, "Bride Says She Stood by Her Man," *St. Petersburg Times*, Online, August 23, 2001, http://www.sptimes.com/News/082301/news_pf/Citrus/Bride_says_she_stood_.shtml

2 Norman Vincent Peale, "Worth Fighting For," *Guideposts* (February 1977): p. 13.

3 Nathaniel Branden, "Advice That Could Save Your Marriage," *Readers Digest* (October 1985): p. 28.

4 Dale Hanson Bourke, "The Real Meaning of Romance," *Today's*   *Christian Woman* (September/October 1987): p. 5.

To keep your marriage
brimming

With love in the loving cup

Whenever you're wrong,
admit it

Whenever you're right,
shut up!

– Ogden Nash

Chapter 3

Communication: Turning a Problem into a Blessing

Some time ago the Second Baptist Church of Houston, Texas, purchased space on several billboards around the city on which it placed one simple phrase: www.mybadmarriage.com. In six weeks, the website registered 656,315 hits. Visitors encountered several questions, including, "What is the number one problem in your marriage?" One answer got more votes than all others — almost 30 percent of respondents named communication as their worst marital problem.

How are the lines of communication in your own home? When you and your spouse talk, do you get to the heart of the issues facing you? Or has

something gone wrong in your communication?

The Plague of Miscommunication

A man once asked his wife what she would like for her 40th birthday. "I'd love to be six again," she replied.

So on the morning of her birthday, the man got her up bright and early, and off they went to a local theme park. What a day! He put her on every ride in the park: the Death Slide, the Screaming Loop, the Wall of Fear, everything. Five hours later, she staggered out of the park, her head reeling and her stomach upside-down.

They got in the car and drove to a McDonald's, where her husband ordered her a Happy Meal, along with extra fries and a refreshing chocolate shake. Then it was off to a movie — the latest Disney — and at last she wobbled home with her giddy husband. Finally, she collapsed in bed.

Her husband leaned over and lovingly asked her, "Well, dear, how was it being six again?"

Popping one bleary eye open, she said, "You idiot! I meant my dress size!"

The wag who told this story added, "The moral of this story is that when a woman speaks and a man is actually listening, he will *still* get it wrong."

Effective communication between a husband and a wife isn't easy! It takes work.

> *When we value things over people, a great deal of miscommunication occurs . . .*

Recently I read an article titled, "Why We Divorce," by Dr. Donald E. Wetmore, president of the Productivity Institute. He writes, "In my experience, 95 percent of all divorces are caused by one thing: a lack of communication. The average working business professional spends, on average, just two minutes per day in meaningful communication with their spouse."[1]

No marriage can thrive and grow in an environment in which spouses spend just two minutes a day in meaningful conversation. That kind of radical deficiency can't help but breed misunderstanding and hard feelings.

Sometimes, we fail to communicate more often

because we fear we'll just be misunderstood. So why bother? And why does miscommunication occur? What so often causes us to miss the meaning our spouse intends to send? I see at least four reasons for miscommunication, all of which give us fits.

1. Poor priorities

Miscommunication happens when we hold poor priorities, and poor priorities in a relationship occur most often when we value "stuff" over the person. That's exactly what's happening today all over America.

It's not the first time men and women have made such a foolish choice, of course. In ancient Israel, they were doing the same thing. So the prophet Isaiah declared to them, "Woe to you who add house to house and join field to field till no space is left and you live alone in the land" (Isa. 5:8).

When we value things over people, a great deal of miscommunication occurs — and our relationships suffer because of it. One key to good communication is to learn how to build up your mate and encourage him or her and do what you can to help him or her become successful. That shows that you value the person over things . . . and with such good priorities in place, effective communication becomes much easier.

2. Poor timing

How many times have you said the right thing to someone, but chose exactly the wrong time to say it? Suppose you really need to talk to your spouse about the leaking picture window in the living room — a good and necessary thing to discuss — but you broach the subject right after your mate starts cuddling and nibbling on your ear lobe late at night while in bed?

The right timing is crucially important. Especially if you want to confront or admonish your spouse, pay careful attention to the timing. Many times, we feel so committed to the truth that we forget about the optimal timing of when that truth can best be spoken.

Jesus recognized this principle and acted on it. That's why, as the time for His crucifixion drew near, He told His men, "I still have many things to say to you, but you cannot bear them now" (John 16:12). Did He dump the whole truckload of truth on them anyway? No, He didn't. What He had yet to say was both true and important, but the timing wasn't right. So He saved the truth for later. We need to master the same art.

For good reason, our culture has a maxim that declares, "Timing is everything." So watch the timing.

3. Poor communication

It may sound obvious, but poor communication causes miscommunication. Both improper words and improper body language can cause serious misunderstanding.

Some people have a knack for cloaking a good intent in a bad message. All of us who preach probably have heard some form of the "compliment" a friend of mine received after serving as a guest speaker at a church. Someone he knew only slightly approached him and said, "You know, I wouldn't have enjoyed that nearly so much if I didn't know you." Ummm . . . well, thanks. I guess.

On the other hand, have you ever dealt with someone who said "the

> *"Timing is everything."*

right thing," and you were saying "the right thing" in response, but their body language showed that they did not truly understand the message you intended to send? Very probably, they immediately took on a defensive posture. They quickly struck back with antagonistic body language, even before they did so with words.

Whether it comes via improper language or improper body posture, poor communication leads to miscommunication. And that's why we have to be very careful to guard both our words and our body language.

4. Poor listening

A lot of us really struggle with the skill of listening. We say we listen, but in fact, often we're just keeping quiet as we compose in our minds what we want to say next.

> *A lot of us really struggle with the skill of listening.*

Do you work to focus on what your spouse is trying to tell you? Poor listening occurs when we become unfocused or distracted. Sometimes it happens because, if we're honest, we just feel very disinterested in what the other is saying.

In the past few months, I've tried to get better at this skill. If I'm doing something and my wife wants to tell me something, I ask her to wait until I'm finished before she begins talking about the matter, so that I can give her my full attention. I know that if I am going to give her words the full weight they merit, I have to finish where I am and start where she wants me to start.

Recently I read an article called "Are You Listening?" by Mike and Marlene Nikolich. They write, "Being listened to is perhaps the most important single factor in a good marriage. Listening entails experiencing what the other person is going through. And listening means that you are interested in the other person."

Did you catch that? Listening involves the emotions; through effective listening, you experience what the other person is saying. Listening also shows that you are interested in that person. It says to him or her, "You matter to me, and so does what you have to say."

When I was growing up, many godly people

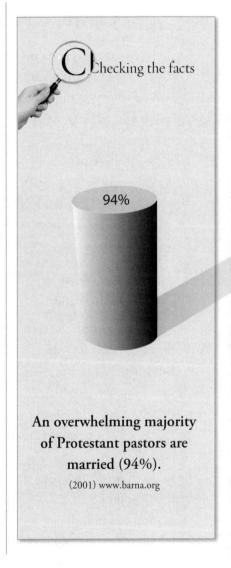

Checking the facts

94%

An overwhelming majority of Protestant pastors are married (94%).

(2001) www.barna.org

reminded me of a good insight: "God has given you two ears and one mouth. You ought to listen twice as much as you talk."

I still think that's a good statement, one which, when followed, cannot help but to improve our communication.

The Key Verse on Communication

At first glance, the text that I consider the key Bible verse on communication seems to have little to do with communication. But looks can be deceiving. Actually, it has everything to do with effective communication.

You can find the key verse on communica-

tion in Ephesians 4:27, which advises us, "Nor give place to the devil."

Believe me, you're headed for trouble if you don't recognize that Satan will do everything he can to warp and distort your communication with your spouse! If you give place to the devil — especially, if you allow a disagreement to fester and grow and create bitter feelings that you fail to deal with before your head hits the pillow at night — then you're headed for hard times. All your communication will be poisoned with the hateful venom of Satan.

Have you ever tried to trace a rumor? It's tough, almost impossible. Do you know why? It's because the author of every rumor in the mill is Satan. He is a liar, a deceiver, and an abuser of words. He is an evil crafts-man who knows how to build up vain imaginations in your mind. If you are not careful, he will ruin your marriage by prompt-ing all sorts of miscommu-nication between you and your spouse.

So refuse to give place to the devil. Refuse to let your arguments and disagreements spill over from day to day, without trying to find resolution. If you let the sun go down on your anger, you're giving the devil a place to build a foothold in your life. Before you know it, he'll

have constructed all sorts of harsh fortresses and wicked outposts that will not allow

> *. . . refuse to give place to the devil.*

healthy words and conver-sations to travel between you and your mate. When you give place to the devil, you make healthy com-munication impossible. And the result is not only unhealthy, it's distinctly unpleasant. So don't let it happen.

Three Ultimate Goals in Communication

The Bible has a lot to say about healthy commu-nication. Perhaps one of the best ways to discover its wisdom is to try to identify some ultimate goals for effective communication. I believe Proverbs 15:1–4 suggests at least three ultimate goals in communication:

A soft answer
turns away wrath,
but a harsh word

> . . . *God calls us to respond properly, by consciously calling on the power of the Holy Spirit of God to give us soft answers . . .*

stirs up anger. The tongue of the wise uses knowledge rightly, but the mouth of fools pours forth foolishness. The eyes of the LORD are in every place, keeping watch on the evil and the good. A wholesome tongue is a tree of life, but perverseness in it breaks the spirit.

1. Respond properly.

Proverbs 15:1 describes a proper response. It tells us to give a soft answer, a strategy that tends to defuse hot circumstances. In the Bible's terms, it "turns away wrath." A harsh answer has the opposite effect. It can create a furor, a wildfire, with the power to devastate and destroy. When we respond with harshness, what usually erupts? Anger. Wrath. Bitterness.

Look back over your own marriage, and see if this pattern hasn't played out between you and your spouse. When did you most often incite the wrath of your mate? Probably, when you responded harshly to some question or criticism. What might have happened, do you think, had you chosen to respond less aggressively and with more grace?

We have to admit it. There are times that, in the midst of our marital disputes, we enjoy playing the devil's advocate. In certain circumstances, we love to give our flesh free reign.

It feels good, in a perverse sort of way, to stir things up. And if we know we're not going to get our way, we just keep it stirred.

But what happens then? We create anger in our own heart as well as anger in the soul of our mate. That's why God calls us to respond properly, by consciously calling on the power of the Holy Spirit of God to give us soft answers even to harsh questions or unfair criticism.

Remember, you cannot control most of what happens to you or what others say to you. But you most certainly *can* control your response to what happens and what is said. And that's all God asks you to control, with His help.

2. Speak wisely

God wants us to learn to speak wisely, because if we do not make this a priority, something else very naturally comes out of our mouths: foolishness. That's what Proverbs 15:2 tells us. "The tongue of the wise uses knowledge rightly, but the mouth of fools pours forth foolishness."

And what does it mean to speak wisely? The Book of Proverbs leaves us in no doubt about the origin of this ability to speak wisely. It tells us, "The fear of the LORD is the beginning of knowledge, but fools despise wisdom and instruction" (Proverbs 1:7).

If we're not in the habit of speaking wisely, then the place to begin to correct this fault is to start meditating on the character and greatness of God — His

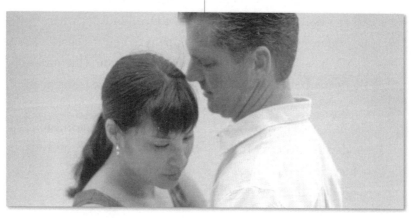

holiness, His power, His wisdom, His love. As we focus more and more on who He is, a proper "fear of the Lord" begins to take root in our souls — and along with it, wisdom. So Proverbs 15:3 reminds us, "The eyes of the LORD are in every place, keeping watch on the evil and the good."

When we remember this, the truth naturally influences how we speak and listen. Neglect to do that, however, and the only option is foolishness.

Have you ever heard anyone speak foolishly? Just listen to yourself sometime — you're bound to hear it! In the heat of the moment, we can say some spectacularly foolish things, and I'm no exception.

> *In the heat of the moment, we can say some spectacularly foolish things . . .*

If we remember the Lord before we speak, however, foolishness has a way of dying in our throats. So let me encourage you to speak wisely. Don't let foolishness take a wrecking ball to your communication.

3. Talk tenderly

Speaking tenderly is not easy for any of us, especially for men. Many a man has brought great destruction upon his marriage through rough or unkind words. Women, of course, can do the very same thing, although it tends to be less of a problem for them than it is for men. That's why God calls all of us to speak tenderly to one another: "A wholesome tongue is a tree of life, but perverseness in it breaks the spirit" (Prov. 15:4).

And what happens if we do not speak tenderly to our mate? His or her spirit closes. And once that spirit closes, it is terribly difficult to get it open again. You certainly can't force it to open by demanding, accusing, or attacking.

Again, tenderness is the key. Tenderness can nudge that closed spirit to open once more. And then healthy communication can bless your marriage and, in turn, allow the two of you to bless others.

The Big Challenge

The Bible has no shortage of challenges for us, and the area of communication is no exception. Ephesians 4:29 tells us, "Let no corrupt word proceed out of your mouth, but what is necessary for edification, that it may impart grace to the hearers."

Tenderness can nudge that closed spirit to open once more.

Some of us hear such a verse and respond, "Well, I don't curse. I don't talk in a corrupt manner. Therefore, this passage doesn't apply to me."

Oh, but it does! It applies to all of us. The word translated "corrupt" does not refer merely to profanity or curse words. It means any communication that is foul, rank, rotten, or worthless. It refers to words and messages that tear down rather than build up, spoil rather than preserve. "Corrupt" words might include messages like the following:

- "Did you really have to wear that dress? It makes you look so frumpy."

- "How many times do I have to ask you to clean out the garage? Do I have to get something to clean out your ears?"

- "You're so lazy, some day the dog is going to mistake you for a bone. Except that'll never happen, because you're too fat."

No profanity anywhere in those words — but all kinds of corruption!

We are not merely to refrain from using "corrupt" words, however; the Bible instructs us to choose positive words that "provide grace to the hearer." The word "grace" means to confer a favor, to give pleasure or profit, to bless that person and to benefit the hearer.

Think of it! When you build up someone, you are God's agent of grace to that person's life. And everyone needs encouragement.

A woman named Deborah Detering and her husband, Floyd, reared three daughters and one son. They also served as foster parents to more than 100 children. Where did she learn such a generous, gracious spirit? From her parents. She writes:

> I remember it as sharply as if it had been yesterday. We were finishing a meal — Dad and Mom, my brother and I — and we sat at the table until we had all finished eating as was expected. Whatever arguments we had, whatever mistakes had been made, it felt good to be a family and to be together. We scraped the last of the chocolate pudding from our bowls and drank the last of our milk. Mom reached for an empty dish before standing up, and Dad took her hand in his, saying, "Thank you, Dear, for another excellent meal." They smiled at each other as if they had just discovered love.

I must have seen that brief scene thousands of times as I grew up, that short grip of hands and the way they looked at each other. It became a symbol of their relationship, and of what my brother and I work for in our own marriages.

It said to us, "Our marriage is a sharing: One of us works in an office and the other cooks; one of us makes money for groceries and the other buys them; each of us appreciates the work the other does; and even when we work separately, we are working together."[2]

Those are words that build up. Those are words that encourage. Those are words that give life. And out of such words do we construct patterns of healthy communication.

When you build up someone, you are God's agent of grace to that person's life.

The 4:32 Rules

I'd like to close this chapter on communication by citing what I call the 4:32 Rules. It's an outstanding principle for each of us to remember and practice in our marriages.

Ephesians 4:32 says, "And be kind to one another, tender-hearted, forgiving one another, even as God in Christ Jesus, forgave you." Consider each of the 4:32 Rules and think of ways to apply all three of them in your own marriage.

If I could do anything over again in my marriage, it would be to express more tenderness.

1. Be kind

It might sound like a simple instruction to be kind, but often it's hard to follow. It's hard to be kind, for example, when your spouse is not kind to you. And yet the Apostle instructs us to be kind.

To be kind means to be good, to be benevolent. Are you good to your spouse? Do you treat him or her well? Are you benevolent toward your mate? Do you give more than you take?

Try a little kindness, and see what it does for your communication between you and your spouse. At the least, you know it couldn't hurt!

2. Be tender

We've already talked about being tender, but it doesn't hurt to repeat good instruction. I think of the words of the apostle Peter here: "I will not be

negligent to remind you always of these things, though you know and are established in the present truth. Yes, I think it is right, as long as I am in this tent, to stir you up by reminding you" (2 Pet. 1:12–13).

Maybe I consider this a good idea because I, at least, need it. May I pull back the drape on the life of Ronnie Floyd? If I could do anything over again in my marriage, it would be to express more tenderness. To be tender means to be compassionate, to act and speak in a sensitive and gentle way, and to do so intentionally and with genuine emotion.

I know personally how very hard it can be to act and speak in a tender way — but be tender! Work to be tender; pray to be

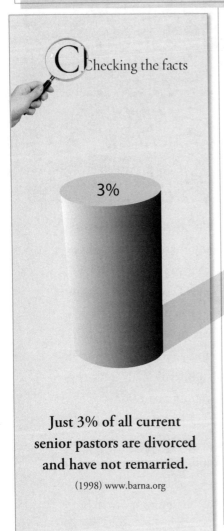

C**hecking the facts**

3%

**Just 3% of all current
senior pastors are divorced
and have not remarried.**

(1998) www.barna.org

tender. When you are not tender, you close the spirit of your mate — and you grieve the Spirit of God. So the apostle Paul gives a special word, particularly to husbands: "Husbands, love your wives and do not be harsh with them" (Col. 3:19; NIV).

Be tender!

3. Be forgiving

Forgiveness has to be a part of your marriage, and therefore a part of your communication. God calls us to exercise grace in freely forgiving others, just like Jesus does with us. He forgives us, He forgets, He moves on, He doesn't bring it up again.

Jesus dropped the charges against you. So guess what? You, too, should drop the charges you might have against your mate.

My experience as a pastor tells me that while men tend to struggle most with being kind and tender, women tend to struggle most in this area of forgiving. If that doesn't describe you, I'm glad. But if it does, please hear what the 4:32 Rules are saying to you.

Jesus dropped the charges! And because Jesus dropped the charges, who am I to hold Jeana hostage? Who am I? I'm not anyone. I need to practice forgiveness in my marriage, regardless of what has been said or done to me.

And you need to do the same.

Don't let poor communication or miscommunication derail your trip to a happy marriage.

Let The Friendship Continue

No marriage can grow strong without its partners working to develop healthy patterns of communication. Don't let poor communication or miscommunication derail your trip to a happy marriage. Please don't let it be said of you, as a church bulletin said of one young couple, "Irving Jones and

Jessie Brown were married on October 24. So ends a friendship that began in school days."[3]

Instead, let the friendship continue. Do all you can to nurture it and strengthen it. And make sure that your communication helps you to achieve that crucial goal.

Endnotes

1 Donald Wetmore, "Why We Divorce," www.salesvantage.com/news/time/why_divorce.shtml

2 Deborah L. Detering, "Mom and Dad Held Hands," unknown source.

3 From a Watertown, Massachusetts, church bulletin.

> . . . let the friendship continue. Do all you can to nurture it and strengthen it.

Marriage is a journey toward
an unknown destination
— the discovery that people
must share not only what
they don't know about each
other, but what they
don't know about themselves.

– Michael Ventura

Chapter 4

How Do We Decide?

HOW do you make decisions in your household? When one of you wants a blue sofa, and the other wants a red loveseat, what procedure do you use to decide what to do? How do decisions generally get made in your marriage?

If problems in communication tend to give married couples the most trouble, then problems in decision-making likely come in a close second. Why? Because the two are closely related. If you don't know how to communicate well, you probably don't know how to make good decisions together. And if you're always fighting about how to make decisions, or who makes them, or what decisions get made,

Seven Decision-Making Questions

1. Did this opportunity begin with God?

If the fear of the Lord is the beginning of wisdom, then a consultation with the Lord is the beginning of good decision-making. When you have a decision to make about this or that opportunity, ask yourselves, "Did we seek this, or did God just bring it to us? Did someone else put it in our hearts, or has God put it in our hearts?" The opportunity may be important. But you have to ask yourselves, as a team, "Is this us, or is this God?"

First Thessalonians 5:24 promises, "He who calls you is faithful, who will also do it." So, who put this thing in your heart? If

then probably your communication is going to suffer badly. The one tends to play off of the other.

So in this chapter, I'd like to offer seven questions to guide your decision-making. They won't help solve all your problems in this area, but they'll surely go a long way toward getting the two of you on the same page.

God is the one putting it in your heart, *He* is calling you.

But someone may ask, "Okay, but does God call us to *all* decisions? Does He have an opinion on every little thing?" I believe that God calls us to most of the major decisions in our life; the problem is that we're not listening. The trouble is that we're too busy to slow down and

> *Sometimes it takes more faith to remain where you are than it does to go where you've never been.*

shut up and ask God what He might want us to do. At other times, quite honestly,

we just don't care. We want what we want, and whether God might have an opinion on it has no place in our deliberations.

But we can't afford such an approach in our marriages. We had better ask ourselves, "Did this begin with God? Is God calling us, or are we simply calling ourselves to do this?"

Who knows how many disasters we get ourselves into, simply because we don't first take the time to ask God whether He has an opinion on the matter before us?

Many of the calamities that devastated ancient Israel occurred because the people of God forgot to inquire of God before they made some decision or took some action.[1] Let's not make the same mistake.

2. Are we willing to do it?

What a big question this is! "Are we willing to do what God seems to be bringing our way? And if He's not bringing it our way, are we willing to walk away from it?" As a couple, you have to ask yourselves this question.

If God calls you to this or that decision, then He wants you to be willing to follow through. Sometimes it takes more faith to remain where you are than it does to go where you've never been.

Jesus once taught that if we really want to know His doctrine — if we want to know His will for us — then we must be willing to do it, whatever it is. He often will not show us where He wants us to go until we demonstrate that we are willing to go there, wherever it might be (John 5).

Are you wondering about what God's will for you might be in this situation or that circumstance? First, you have to ask yourself, *Am I willing to do whatever God shows me?* God wants us to kneel before Him and say, "Lord, I am willing to do whatever you want me to do. And Lord, that means whatever you ask me to do, whether it's to stay or it's to go. Whether it's to do this thing or to do that thing, I am willing to do it. And

Checking the facts

12%

Only one out of every eight pastors (12%) have ever experienced a divorce and most pastors who have been divorced have since been remarried.

(2001) www.barna.org

whatever you're asking me to do, the answer is yes. I'm available. I'm here."

3. Is it God's timing?

Ecclesiastes 3 discusses the timing issue. It begins, "To everything there is a season, and a time for every purpose under heaven: A time to be born, and a time to die; a time to plant, and a time to pluck what is planted. . . ."

The big, sovereign God we serve has a timetable for events and activities that take place throughout His vast realm. One of the most challenging things in life is to understand that *your* timetable is not always *God's* timetable.

Guess what? God may have put this thing in your heart. Guess what? You may be willing to do it. But guess what else? It may not be the right time yet. It doesn't matter what the issue may be: having children, buying a house, moving to another area. You have to take into consideration God's timing.

So you must ask yourself, "Are we willing to wait on God? Do we want God's timing in our marriage?" Keep in mind that God may say to you, "I'm going to let you do it, but it's just not the right time."

You have to take into consideration God's timing.

4. What is the biblical grid of James 3:13–18 saying to us?

James 3:13–18 presents a great "decision-making grid" that helps believers to work through tough decisions. The passage essentially contrasts human wisdom with divine wisdom and describes the primary characteristics of each. You will get the most help from this grid by working through the passage on your own, but note the main contrasts it describes between human wisdom and God's wisdom:

How Do We Decide?

James Decision Making Grid

Human wisdom	God's wisdom
Bitter envy	Pure
Self-seeking	Willing to yield
Self-justifying	Without hypocrisy
Evil possibilities	Good fruits
Earthly	Gentle
Unspiritual	Full of mercy
Confusion	Peace
Demonic (double minded)	Unwavering

How many of us make decisions without reference to the peace of God?

When you're struggling with some decision you have to make, work through this grid. Ask yourselves, "Are we confused? Or do we feel peace about this? Do we waver every day as to what we should do, or do we have a sense of conviction about it? Do we want this because it benefits us, or do we want this because we believe God will use it to expand the kingdom of God through us?"

Working through this decision-making grid can rule out something because it doesn't appear to be of God, or it might be God's voice to you, God's cheerleader to urge you on to what you believe God wants you to do. But in either case, you're making your decisions based on the Word of God.

We must be willing to put every decision we make through the grid of James 3. If you've trusted in the book to give you reliable information about how to get to heaven, then you ought to trust it enough to tell you how to get to the decisions in this life that best honor God.

5. Does this decision demonstrate the fruit of the Holy Spirit?

Galatians 5:22–23 tells us, "But the fruit of the Spirit is love, joy, peace, longsuffering, kindness, goodness, faithfulness, gentleness, and self-control." So ask yourselves this question: does this decision demonstrate the fruit of the Holy Spirit in our lives?

In other words, how does love factor in on this decision? How is the joy factor? If you feel miserable, it's probably not God's will. Or how about peace? How many of us make decisions without reference to the peace of God? How is the longsuffering factor? Have we patiently waited for the will of God? How is the kindness factor? How is the goodness factor? How is the faithfulness factor or the gentleness factor or the self-control factor? Does our decision demonstrate the fruit of the Holy Spirit?

6. Does this decision bring glory to God?

Suppose you feel like letting your mate really have it. Does that bring glory to God? Or you really feel like doing something that you know might cause a division within the family. Does that bring glory to God? "I think the Lord wants us to move into this house." Well, would the move bring glory to God? It might depend on how you want to use it. "Does the Lord want me to do this big business deal?" Listen, it's not about conquering multiple millions; it's about understanding that God has gifted you and equipped you with skills and talents, not simply to help your personal portfolio, but to increase God's

eternal portfolio for the kingdom of God.

First Corinthians 10:31 says, "Therefore, whatever you eat or drink or whatever you do, do all to the glory of God."

And that includes decision-making.

7. What is God saying to me?

After you work through the biblical grid together, and after you ask yourselves these difficult first six questions, being as honest as you can, finally you should ask, "What is God saying to us?"

Is this God's best for you? Many of us live with a lot less than God's best, all because we're not willing to wait and trust and have faith in God and in what He wants for us. That's why some of us have gotten

> *. . . it's not about conquering multiple millions . . .*

divorces; that's why some are in debt; that's why some feel miserable in their jobs — and the list goes on and on.

Sometimes, God speaks so clearly about an issue that you both just know in your hearts that it's the right thing to do. But not every decision is that easy.

I have found it wise to listen to an old adage: "When in doubt, don't." Why not? Because doubt creates confusion and doubt creates a wavering spirit. So Paul writes, "Whatever is not from faith is sin" (Rom. 14:23).

I'm firmly convinced that God treats us like a loving father. Sometimes when your heart is right and you're willing to do whatever God wants you to do, God looks at you and says, "I tell you son, I tell you daughter, those are two

> *I'm firmly convinced that God treats us like a loving father.*

great choices. You just do whatever you want to do."

You Want to Win Big

Ten years ago, Luke Perry, then a star on a popular TV show and a rising film celebrity, was asked about the decisions he made in his career and the risks he took.

"The funny thing about risk," he replied, "is that the only way to win big is to bet big. Marriage is the biggest bet one can make. I want to do it only once, and I want to win big."[2]

Do you want to win big in marriage? You'll greatly increase your odds of that happening, not by engaging in risky behavior, but by submitting your decision-making to the will and pleasure of God. If you do that, and if you do so together, you'll win bigger than all the hordes who stream to Las Vegas, looking for lady luck.

In fact, you won't need luck at all. Why not? Because you'll have golden wisdom straight from the treasure vaults of heaven.

Talk about winning big!

Endnotes

1   See, for example, Joshua 9:14; 1 Chronicles 10:14; 13:3; 15:13.

2   *Parade* (February 20, 1994): p. 28.

Before you marry, keep your two eyes open; after you marry, shut one.

– Jamaican proverb

Chapter 5

Don't Forget the Romance

MY long-lost cousin from Alabama, Ronney, showed up one Sunday at church just before I spoke to the congregation about romance in marriage. He figured he could give our men a few pointers that would help their marriages really sizzle. He called it his "Top Ten List on Mullet Romance." See if any of them might help your own marriage:

Number 10: Bring home a nice bouquet of moon pies and a cold bottle of RC Cola.

Number 9: Always compliment her muumuu and her house shoes.

Number 8: Grill out a juicy piece of Spam.

explained. "I'm not paying no 39 dollars for no pair of underwear. No, head right down to Family Dollar and get you a three pack.")

Number 4: Plan a chicken wing and root beer picnic.

Number 3: Braid the kids' rat-tails and mullets before school, because your sweetie's got a lot going on; you want to help her.

Number 7: Grab your sweetie and slow dance to the national anthem, "Sweet Home Alabama."

Number 6: Spruce up the RV and head on out to a Nascar race.

Number 2: Dedicate a song to her at the bowling ally; anything by Def Lepard or Bon Jovi will work.

Number 1: Take her out for an all-you-can-eat buffet at the local greasy spoon. ("Where else you gonna get salad bar, potato bar, spaghetti, chicken

Number 5: Buy her some intimate apparel. ("And I'm not talking about no Victoria Secret, either," he

nuggets, corn nuggets, steak, hamburgers, and swirly ice cream with sprinkles on it for only 6.99?" he asked.)

Well, that's one way to look at romance. But I think it might be a lot more helpful to consider what God has to say on the subject. And I think it would be particularly helpful to see how the Lord illustrates what He's talking about.

God Endorses Romance

Did you know that God believes in romance? He really does! He believes in a husband and a wife experiencing romance together.

In fact, God not only believes in romance, He ordains it. He is the one behind romance and He is the one who encourages romance. It's not too much to say that God wants you to experience the full reality of who He created you to be — and part of that is to enjoy true romance in marriage.

The clearest biblical illustration we have of romance and the important place it has in any successful marriage is found in the little book we know as the Song of Solomon.

. . . God not only believes in romance, He ordains it.

Stage One: Premarital Romance

The first two chapters of the Song of Solomon picture for us what godly premarital romance is like. It suggests four characteristics about this stage of romance.

1. Affirmation

In the Song of Solomon, the man is known as "the beloved," while the woman is called "the Shulamite." Notice what the man says to the object of his affection: "Behold, you are fair, my love. Behold, you are fair and you have dove's eyes" (Song of Sol. 1:15).

Twice he calls her "fair." The word in the original Hebrew means beautiful or lovely. And he tells her that she has "dove's eyes." The dove is known for its gentleness; he sees gentleness in her eyes. Also, it is said that doves have but one love for a lifetime.

Don't miss how he affirms both her and her appearance. Guys, do you want to know how to romance a girl? You start by affirming her.

2. Attraction

Not surprisingly, the Shulamite feels very attractive to this complimentary male. Her positive response suggests a principle: attraction usually follows affirmation. Without affirmation, attraction almost never follows. Women like it when their suitors say things like, "That sure is a nice outfit you have on today." They do not like it so well when they say, "Man, you got big feet."

In the 16th verse of chapter one we learn how the Shulamite responds to her suitor's words: "Behold, you are handsome, my beloved. Yes, pleasant! Also our bed is green."

She thinks he's handsome! And pleasant! When she speaks of their "green bed," she has in mind the carpet of the field; that's where they walk and court one another, on the cool, green grass of the field.

A little later she gets to talking with her girlfriends — girlfriends do talk, guys, just so you know — and hear what she says: "He brought me to the ban-

queting house, and his banner over me was love. Sustain me with cakes of raisins, refresh me with apples, for I am lovesick" (Song of Sol. 2:4–5).

Isn't that great? Maybe you didn't even know this was in the Bible. But you haven't seen anything yet!

"His left hand is under my head, and his right hand embraces me" (Song of Sol. 2:6). And then she addresses her girlfriends directly: "I charge you, O daughters of Jerusalem, by the gazelles or by the does of the field, do not stir up nor awaken love until it pleases" (Song of Sol. 2:7).

Do you know what she's saying? "I've waited my whole life to be loved like this! And I'm telling you, my friends, I'm love sick."

This girl didn't compromise her convictions; she waited. And God rewarded her! She was telling her friends, "This gorgeous guy swept me off of my feet with his romance!" How could she not feel attracted to him?

3. Fidelity

"My beloved is mine," the Shulamite says, "and I am his" (Song of Sol. 2:16). That means she was faithful to him, and he was faithful to her. They practiced fidelity toward each other.

I like to say to every young woman and every young man I meet that if your boyfriend or girlfriend isn't faithful to you in your courtship, he or she will not be faithful to you after

> . . . *if your boyfriend or girlfriend isn't faithful to you in your courtship, he or she will not be faithful to you after marriage.*

marriage. So take a hint! Don't suppose, "Well, he's just getting his wild oats sown." If he is, just let him go sow them with someone else; you get away from him. You don't want any part of a man or of a woman who cannot remain faithful even in the courtship stage!

4. Initiation

"My beloved spoke," the Shulamite reported, "and he said to me, 'rise up, my love, my fair one, and come away. For lo, the winter has passed and the rain is over and gone' " (Song of Sol. 2:10–11).

Isn't that beautiful? There is nothing like God's Word!

Her beau invited her to come away with him — he initiated the romance. Do you realize what he was doing? He was proposing marriage. That's what he meant when he said "come away with me."

This romantic idea never grows old. As I write,

the 24-year-old singer, Norah Jones, is redefining the music industry. It is amazing. She crosses all borders, from jazz to folk, bass, pop, soul, and country. In fact, she is erasing musical boundaries. She began singing in a church choir at age five in Grapevine, Texas. And now she has become an incredible songwriter, arranger, and singer.

Norah won a Grammy award for her incredible song, "Come Away With Me." It's a love song — and its roots run clear back to these words in the Song of Solomon.

I tell you, God ordains romance.

> *There might be 100 women out there a man could marry, but there's one who is perfect for him.*

That's why it continues to top the charts in every age.

Stage Two: Marital Romance

So the beloved proposes and the Shulamite accepts. They get married. And then what happens? Does the romance stop?

Hardly. Now notice the chief characteristics of marital romance.

1. Affirmation and attraction

The man loves the Shulamite after they are married in the same way he loved her before they get married! "You are all fair, my love, and there is no spot in you," he coos to her. "You are beautiful, my love" (Song of Sol. 4:7).

Do you know what he's saying to her? "You are perfect for me."

That's exactly what Adam, the first man, said about Eve, the first woman. "At last!" he said, "She is part of my own flesh and bone! She will be called 'woman,' because she was taken out of a man" (Gen. 2:23; NLT). The late Ray Stedman commented, "What Adam meant, of course, was, 'Finally, I have found that which completes me, corresponds to me, is equal with me, is sent to help me fulfill the task which God has given me to do.' "[1]

There might be 100 women out there a man could marry, but there's one who is perfect for him. And when he finds her, he has to make sure the affirmation is there to fuel the attraction.

2. Initiation and invitation

The beloved says to his bride, "Come with me from Lebanon, my spouse, with me from Lebanon. Look from the top of Amana, and the top of Senir and Herman, from the lions' dens, from the mountains of the leopards" (Song of Sol. 4:8). The key statement here, of course, is the initiation: "Come away with me." He initiates. He invites her to come.

After you marry, there are times when a man needs to look at his wife and say to her, "Come away with me," even if it is for a single night. And

you know what? You don't need to fight over who ought to do the initiating or who ought to do the inviting. One of you take the lead; the other ought to be smart enough to follow.

Do you want to do romance God's way? Then you need a code word. Here it is: "Hey, sweetie, come away with me." Immediately, she knows what's up. He knows what's up. Just learn to master the code word:

"Come away with me!"

After I had spoken about this, my wife challenged me greatly. One afternoon in my Senior Staff Team Meeting, knocked on the door, interrupted it, they began playing, Nora Jones' song: "Come Away With Me". She captured me when I was least expecting it, had my stuff all packed already, and we headed away that early afternoon for a night away in Branson, Missouri. We were back by noon the next day.

What did Jeana do that day? She made me feel special. She knew I needed to be away due to schedule, but her goal was to make that day very special beyond the norm. She accomplished her goal.

It does not matter whether the husband or the wife leads in this, but what matters is someone makes the other feel special. If you miss the code word: "Come away with me!" you may miss one cool experience with your mate. Let the music begin in your marriage . . . now.

You don't need to fight over who ought to do the initiating or who ought to do the inviting.

3. Intimacy and interest

The beloved then says to his wife, "You have ravished my heart, my sister, my spouse; you have ravished my heart with one look of your eyes and one link of your necklace" (4:9).

What does the phrase mean, "ravished my heart"? He means "you have put heart back into me; you have made me want to come alive." How did she do that? Through her love, openly expressed to him. Men sometimes give the impression that they don't need to know of their spouse's love. But take a cue from this woman, ladies; men need to know that you love them.

A woman has the power to make a man come alive with her love.

A woman has the power to make a man come alive with her love. So if you feel your husband is dead, force him back to life with your love. Love him even when he is unlovable. Don't hold back; that's the point. With one look of your eyes or with that special way that you present yourself to him, you put heart back into him. And men can't be all they are supposed to be without heart.

Do you see that he calls his wife, "sister"? He's not a pervert; in the ancient near eastern world, a man would often use the term "sister" to express three things to his wife: endearment, closeness, and permanence. And so Solomon was saying to his young bride, "you're mine forever. I want to be close to you, I'm endeared

to you and I feel close to you."

But it doesn't stop there. "A garden closed is my sister, my spouse, a spring shut up, a fountain sealed," he says in verse 12. "A fountain of gardens, a well of living waters and streams from Lebanon," he calls her in verse 15.

Why is he suddenly talking about a garden? Well, he's not, exactly. His wife's body is the garden.

Prior to marriage, she had shut him out of her garden; that is what a woman is supposed to do before marriage. But there is great power in that garden! He declares it full of fountains and waters and streams. He is telling her that she looks wonderful and ravishing. He is expressing his intense interest in her, declaring that he craves intimacy with her. Not sexual intimacy alone, but also emotional and spiritual intimacy.

4. Experience and ecstasy

"Awake, O north wind, and come, O south!" the Shulamite commands. "Blow upon my garden, that its spices may flow out. Let my beloved come to his garden and eat its pleasant fruits" (Song of Sol. 4:16).

Isn't that good? That ought to get a man fired up! And if it doesn't fire him up, then something's wrong with him. Notice especially that she invites him into her garden.

Then it's the man's turn. "I have come to my garden, my sister, my spouse; I have gathered my myrrh with my spice; I have eaten my honeycomb with my honey; I have drunk my wine with my milk" (Song of Sol. 5:1).

What is he saying? He means, "When I experience her, I will have ecstasy."

And that's what they both wanted prior to marriage! They longed to consummate the fullness of their love through sexual intercourse.

Notice, they hold nothing back. They give themselves to one another, fully. This is the consummation of their romance. All of the love, all of the emotion, all of the intimacy — it is now brought to a high climax, the ultimate, biblical result of true romance.

Your marriage needs this! So does mine. You

were meant for it. God means for you to have it and enjoy it.

So all I can add is . . . happy gardening!

Come Away With Me

How is your marriage doing these days? Is it vibrant, growing, healthy? Is it stable, solid, steady? Or has it suffered through some tremors or rough seas lately? Have the embers grown cold and dark?

God wants your marriage not only to survive tough times, but to thrive and become a beautiful example of His grace and power even in a wicked age. So God says to you, even as He instructs you to say to your mate, "Come away with me."

> *God wants your marriage not only to survive tough times, but to thrive and become a beautiful example of His grace and power even in a wicked age.*

Remember, God himself is the author of romance.

So God says to you today, "Come away with Me, and I will heal your marriage."

"Come away with Me, and wait with Me until I bring health and hope to your union."

"Come away with Me, and in due time and at the proper season, we will work together to make things right."

Do you need to come away with Him today? Do you need a special touch from His hand? Do you need the special comfort of His Spirit and the warm counsel of His Son?

If so, then go with Him. Don't delay. Do it now. Go with Him for your marriage's sake. Go with Him for your own sake. And perhaps, if you listen closely enough, you will hear His call to you, the one he loves so dearly:

> Make haste, my beloved, and be like a gazelle or a young stag on the mountains of spices (Song of Sol. 8:14).

Endnotes

1 Ray Stedman, Peninsula Bible Church Discovery Papers, catalog no. 3769.

Don't delay. Do it now. Go with Him for your marriage's sake.

Marriage is like twirling a baton, turning handsprings or eating with chopsticks. It looks easy until you try it.

– Helen Rowland, quoted by Robert Keeler in The Toastmaster, *Reader's Digest, June, 1994, p. 130*

PHOTO CREDITS

Also by Dr. Ronnie Floyd . . .

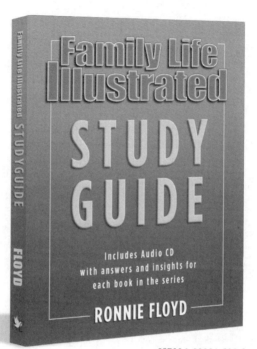

ISBN 0-89221-599-2

<u>Special Features Include:</u>
- Study questions in each book for reflection and to aid
  small-group study
- Study guide that works for all six books that also includes
  an audio CD from Dr. Floyd with answers and insights for
  each book.

5 1/4 x 8 3/8 • Paper • 128 pages
• *INCLUDES AUDIO CD*

Available at Christian bookstores nationwide.

Also by Dr. Ronnie Floyd . . .

ISBN 0-89221-588-7

Your job, your finances, your friends — nothing you ever do will matter as much as being a good parent to your child. Going beyond the surface strategies and quick psycho-babble solutions, this book reveals solid, God-based insight on becoming a more effective parent. Don't choose to struggle alone — tap into the wealth of wisdom God wants to share with you and find how you can make a positive, remarkable, and lasting change in the lives of your children today!

Are you happening to life or is life simply happening to you? Over-whelmed, overworked, stressed, and tired, it's easy to lose sight of things important to you as a woman, wife, and perhaps even a mother. Be empowered, be decisive, and be open to God's gently guiding hand in your life! God can be what you need – He can strengthen, calm, and sustain you when life seems impossible. No matter what you face, God can give you the knowledge and wisdom to adapt, endure, and affect a change!

ISBN 0-89221-583-6

Available at Christian bookstores nationwide.

Also by Dr. Ronnie Floyd . . .

Are you sitting on the sidelines of your family's life? Investing in material goods instead of Christ-like character? You need to make a difference, be a part of, and a leader for your spouse and your children. God is looking for men willing to fight for the future of their families — and be examples of strong Christian leadership within their communities. Don't be irrelevant! Be a God-inspired guide for your family each day!

ISBN 0-89221-584-4

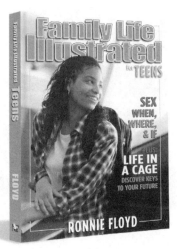

ISBN 0-89221-586-0

It seems like everything keeps changing and no one understands. Every day seems to bring more pivotal decisions to be made. Life is complicated and stressful, and you feel you are alone! Fight the isolation – don't be a spectator in your own life! Get powerful solutions and strategies to survive and thrive during the toughest time of your life — and find out how to rely on God when life overwhelms you!

Available at Christian bookstores nationwide.

Also by Dr. Ronnie Floyd . . .

Money, debt, credit card complications — believe it or not, the Bible can be the most practical guide to financial management you will ever find! Simple, easy-to-implement solutions don't require high cost solutions or painful personal concessions. Don't do without the answers which can help change your financial future and solve a critical area of stress affecting you, your family, or even your marriage. Invest in God's wisdom, and reap the blessings He has in store for you!

ISBN 0-89221-587-9

The Gay Agenda is a compelling and compassionate look at one of the most turbulent issues of our society today – homosexuality and same-sex marriage. Dr. Ronnie Floyd states the importance of maintaining the traditional family, while revealing the homosexual agenda at work in our schools, churches, and government. He also looks at the ongoing controversies over gay clergy, and turns the spotlight on judicial activism as well. Dr. Floyd makes clear the political chaos and confusion of this election-year hot potato as both major parties seek to find political payoffs on these issues. *The Gay Agenda* cannot be ignored.

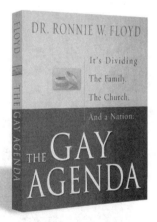

ISBN: 0-89221-582-8

7 x 9 • Casebound • 140 pages

Available at Christian bookstores nationwide.

About the Author . . .

Recognizing the vital importance of the family in the success of not only individuals, but for our society today, the "Family Life Illustrated" series offers real answers for real-life problems being faced each day by families. Articulate, informative, and always relevant — Dr. Ronnie Floyd is reaching the hearts of millions weekly through his broadcast ministry Invitation to Life, aired on WGN's Superstation and other television networks nationally each week. An accomplished author of 17 books as well as a powerful group speaker, Dr. Floyd has over 27 years of ministry experience and is senior pastor for a congregation of 15,000 in Northwest Arkansas. Dr. Floyd has been been seen on Fox News, WorldNetDaily, Janet Parshall's America, Washington Watch, USA Radio Network, FamilyNet, and more!

MORE RESOURCES FROM
DR. RONNIE W. FLOYD

CD/VHS/DVD
"Family Life Illustrated Series"

CD/VHS/DVD
"The Gay Agenda"

Other Books By Dr. Floyd
Life on Fire
How to Pray
The Power of Prayer and Fasting
The Meaning of a Man

Weekly International Television and Internet

Sundays: (7:30 a.m. CST) WGN SUPERSTATION

Thursdays: (9:00 p.m. CST) Daystar Christian Television Network

Sundays: (9:15 a.m. CST) Live webcast on
www.fbcspringdale.org

For more information on all resources: www.invitationtolife.org

For information about our church:
www.fbcspringdale.org   www.churchph.com

or call (479) 751-4523 and ask for Invitation to Life